KB244460

Great Inventions around Us

Happy House

About Wise & Wide

- A systematic 6-level English reading program based on Lexile® measures
- Diverse and interesting topics chosen from the elementary curriculums of Korea and English speaking western countries
- Well-written books in various forms including fiction stories, descriptive texts, and classics retold
- The informative but original fiction stories grab your interest, leading to the easy and clear understanding of the educational content.
- Improve thinking skills with solid after-reading activities at all levels of the series.

Wise & Wide is a 6-level English reading program that consists of 60 books and each level is systematically divided by Lexile® measures. The Lexile® Framework for Reading is the most popular reading measuring system in American formal education curriculums and many English programs. Over 20 out of 50 states in the U.S. mark Lexile® measures directly on students' final report cards and over 300 well-known publishers adopt and use Lexile® measures.

Experience many kinds of readings written by professional writers from the U.S. and England. They used interesting topics that were carefully chosen after analyzing elementary curriculums from around the world including Korea, the U.S., England, and Australia among many others. Comprehensive after-reading activities including graphic organizers, speaking tasks, and After-reading Tests are ready for you.

Levels in the series and their corresponding Lexile® measures

Level	Lexile® measures	U.S. Grade
Level 1	Below 200L	Pre K - K
Level 2	190L - 400L	Lower Grade 1
Level 3	350L - 530L	Upper Grade 1
Level 4	420L - 650L	Grade 2
Level 5	520L - 940L	Grade 3 - 4
Level 6	830L - 1070L	Grade 5 - 6

* Smart Readers: Wise & Wide level 1 is applicable to the preschool level in the U.S.

* The source of the relationship between Lexile® measures and U.S. school grades: CCSS(Common Core State Standards) FOR ENGLISH LANGUAGE ARTS, APPENDIX A (2012, which is used by 45 states in the U.S.)

Topic List

	Level 1	Level 2	Level 3	Level 4	Level 5	Level 6
Book 1	Science›Biology: The hibernation of animals Story	Science›Biology: Living and nonliving things Story	Science›Biology› Animals & the Environment: Sea otters Story	Environment› Living with nature: The diver & the persimmon tree Story	Science›Biology› Animal: Amazing animals of the Amazon Story	Science›Biology: Germs, transmitted diseases Story
Book 2	Literature› World classics: Aesop's fables Story	Literature› Traditional fairy tale: Old tales about stones Story	Social Studies› Economy: To run a business to make and save money Story	Science›Biology› Plants: Photosynthesis Story	Science›Earth science: Earth's layers,earthquakes, volcanoes, and earth's atmosphere Report	Mathematics› Sequence: The golden ratio & the Fibonacci sequence Story
Book 3	Science›Physics: How shadows are formed Story	Literature› World classics: Peter Pan Story	Science›Scientific technology: Nanobots Story	Literature›Myths: World's creation stories Story	Literature› Legend: The story of King Arthur Story	Literature›Myths: Constellation myths Story
Book 4	Literature› Traditional literature: The Talmud Story	Science›Biology› Animal: Polar bears Story	Science›Biology› Animal: Mountain gorillas Story	Social Studies› Cultural anthropology: Amazing ancient cultures of the world Story	Science› Earth science: Clouds and weather Story	Literature› Human & animals: The friendship between a girl and a horse Story
Book 5	Social Studies› Ethics: Rules in daily life Story	Science›Biology: The five senses Report	Social Studies› Cultural anthropology: Astonishing festivals Report	Art›Music: Stories from two operas Story	Social Studies› World culture & history: The Renaissance Story	Sports› Board sports: Surfing & snowboarding Story
Book 6	Social Studies› World geography & travel: Tourist attractions around the world Story	Science›Biology› Animal: Dinosaurs Story	Science› Astronomy: The solar system Story	Social Studies› People: Three great people who overcame hardships Story	Science›Scientific technology: The wonderful world of robots Report	Art›Music: Composers of the Romantic Era Report
Book 7	Science› Space science: The life of astronauts Report	Social Studies› Cultural anthropology: Mythological monsters from around the world Report	Mathematics› Elementary mathematics: Numbers, measurement, shapes and data Report	Science & Social Studies› Technology & culture: Inventions from around the world Report	Art›Works of art: Famous paintings Report	Social Studies› Human & animals: Animals in action for human Report
Book 8	Social Studies› Cultural anthropology: Various living cultures of the world Story	Art›Music: Instruments in the orchestra Story		Social Studies› History: The California Gold Rush Report	Social Studies & Science› Psychology: Psychology in everyday life Story	Literature› World classics: The Merchant of Venice Story
Book 9						
Book 10						

* 10 books in each level will be published.

How to Use This Book

•Before Reading

You can easily find the topic and what kind of story you are about to read.

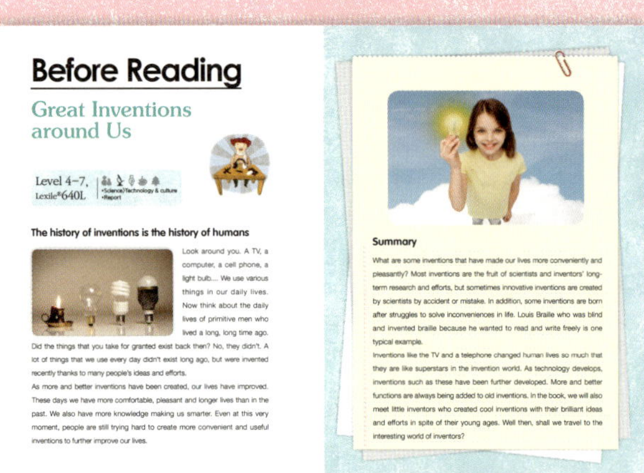

•The text

All the stories were written by professional writers from the U.S. and England, so you will read authentic and appropriate English sentences and expressions in every book in the series.

•Pop Quiz

Check out right away if you understand what you have just read by solving a pop quiz that checks your comprehension.

•Key Words

The key words and expressions on each page are listed for you to easily study them.

•Aha! Tips

Download free Korean explanations at *www.ihappyhouse.co.kr* for all of the sentences marked with "Aha!". These explain cultural, scientific, and economic knowledge or they deal with aspects of English such as grammatical structures or idiomatic expressions. There are lots of "Aha! Tips" to help you understand the text.

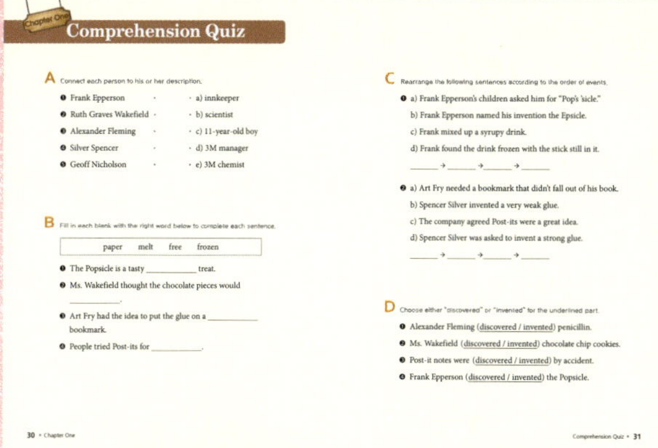

•Comprehension Quiz

After reading one chapter, solve various questions to find out if you fully understand the content.

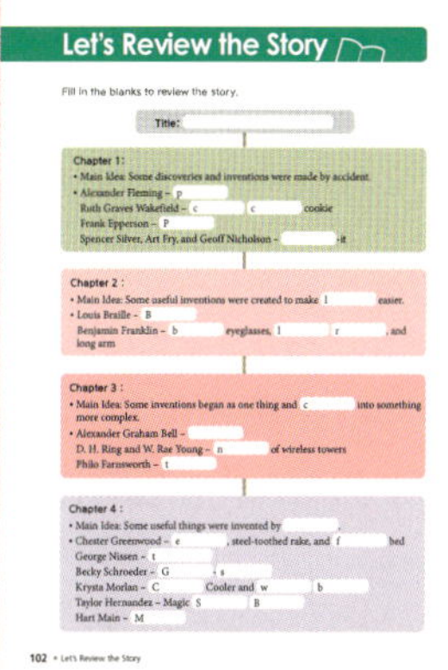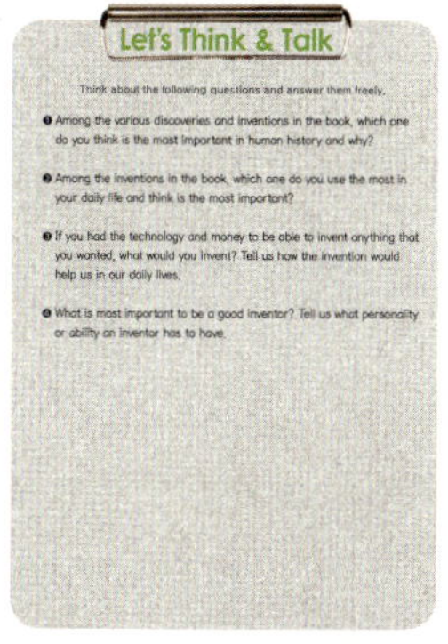

•Let's Review the Story /
•Let's Think & Talk

Fill in the blanks in the organizer to summarize the whole story. Express your own thinking and feelings about the story by answering the questions. You can build up logic and reasoning skills for your essay examinations in the future.

Appendix

Audio CD

In the CD audio book form, the texts are read vividly by American professional voice actors. (MP3 files downloaded for free)

After-reading Test

Solve an additionally provided After-reading Test for each book.

The Korean translation, Answer Keys, a Word Quiz, a Word List, and Aha! Tips for each book

You can download them for free at *www.ihappyhouse.co.kr* or *www.darakwon.co.kr*

Before Reading

Great Inventions around Us

The history of inventions is the history of humans

Look around you. A TV, a computer, a cell phone, a light bulb.... We use various things in our daily lives. Now think about the daily lives of primitive men who lived a long, long time ago.

Did the things that you take for granted exist back then? No, they didn't. A lot of things that we use every day didn't exist long ago, but were invented recently thanks to many people's ideas and efforts.

As more and better inventions have been created, our lives have improved. These days we have more comfortable, pleasant and longer lives than in the past. We also have more knowledge making us smarter. Even at this very moment, people are still trying hard to create more convenient and useful inventions to further improve our lives.

Summary

What are some inventions that have made our lives more conveniently and pleasantly? Most inventions are the fruit of scientists and inventors' long-term research and efforts, but sometimes innovative inventions are created by scientists by accident or mistake. In addition, some inventions are born after struggles to solve inconveniences in life. Louis Braille who was blind and invented braille because he wanted to read and write freely is one typical example.

Inventions like the TV and a telephone changed human lives so much that they are like superstars in the invention world. As technology develops, inventions such as these have been further developed. More and better functions are always being added to old inventions. In the book, we will also meet little inventors who created cool inventions with their brilliant ideas and efforts in spite of their young ages. Well then, shall we travel to the interesting world of inventors?

Great Inventions around Us

Great Inventions around Us

Timeless Inventions

Since the beginning of time, human beings have looked for new ways to do things.

They have found new ways to improve their lives.

They have found ways to make certain tasks easier.

Often, these inventions impact and improve human culture.

Let's talk about the wheel, for example. The wheel did not always exist. Way back in 3500 BC, early man invented the wheel. Ancient peoples

▲ an early form of a wagon

used wheels on chariots and wagons.

Over the centuries, this simple invention has been used in thousands of ways. The wheel has made life easier for humans.

Think of all the ways in which wheels are used today. Can you imagine a world without wheels in it?

KEY WORDS

- timeless
- invention
- since
- human being
- look for
- way
- improve
- life
- certain
- task
- impact
- culture (= civilization)
- wheel
- for example
- always
- exist
- way back
- BC (*cf.* AD)
- early man (= ancient people)
- chariot
- wagon
- century
- simple
- thousands of
- think of
- imagine
- without

Some inventions, like the wheel, have had a big effect on human culture. The wheel changed the way people lived. 

Other inventions, like the Popsicle, have not changed the way people live, but continue to provide pleasure and convenience to people.

We will talk about both types of inventions. We will also talk about the people who invented them.

Did children like you invent anything as important as the wheel? Did children like you invent anything as enjoyable as Popsicles?

Let's take a look.

POP QUIZ

Which invention has changed the world?
ⓐ Popsicles
ⓑ wheels

KEY WORDS

- like
- have an effect on
- Popsicle
- continue
- provide
- pleasure
- convenience
- both

- type
- invent
- children
- as + *Adjective* + as A
- important
- enjoyable
- take a look

Chapter One

Agreeable Accidents

It is important to understand the difference between an invention and a discovery.

An invention is something that never existed until someone imagined and created it.

A discovery is something that already existed and was found.

Penicillin was discovered by Alexander Fleming.

Alexander Fleming was a Scottish scientist.

In 1928 he was researching the flu virus.

He noticed mold growing in a petri dish.

He also saw that the mold was killing bacteria in the petri dish.

Lucky for us he paid attention.

He studied this discovery.

It led to the development of penicillin!

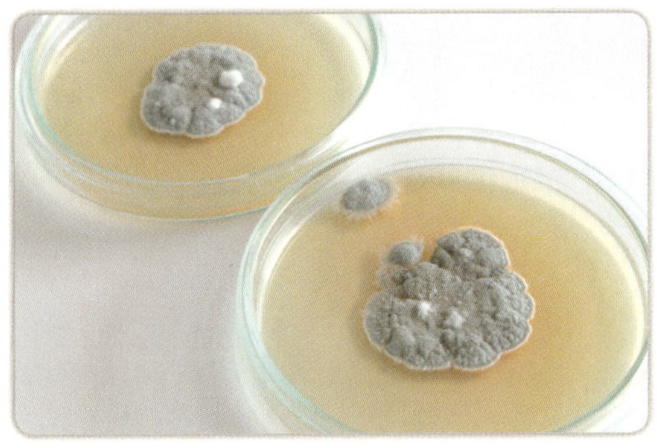

▲ penicillin grown in a petri dish

KEY WORDS

- agreeable
- accident
- difference
- discovery
- something
- until
- create

- already
- find (find-found-found)
- discover
- Scottish
- research
- the flu virus
- notice

- mold
- grow
- petri dish
- bacteria
- pay attention
- lead to (lead-led-led)
- development

Penicillin is a strong
antibiotic.
It cures many infections.
Penicillin existed before
Alexander Fleming
discovered it.
Maybe your doctor gave you
penicillin when you were
sick. The penicillin made you
feel better.
This was a great discovery
by Alexander Fleming.
The discovery of penicillin
has saved many lives.

▲ a poster that promoted the effectiveness of
penicillin during World War II
(See page for author [Public domain],
via Wikimedia Commons)

Just as penicillin was discovered by accident, sometimes inventions are made by accident, too.

Can you think of common items which were invented by accident?

Here are a few: Post-it notes, Popsicles, and the chocolate chip cookie.

Here is how that sweet treat,
the chocolate chip cookie,
was invented.
One evening in 1930,
an innkeeper, Ruth
Graves Wakefield,
decided to bake
cookies.
After she began, she
realized she didn't have any
baking chocolate.
She didn't know what to do. Then she remembered she
had a block of Nestlé semi-sweet chocolate.
She chopped up the block of chocolate to use in place of
the baking chocolate.

KEY WORDS

- sweet treat (*cf.* treat)
- innkeeper
- bake
- realize
- baking chocolate

- remember
- block
- semi-sweet chocolate
- chop up
- in place of

Ms. Wakefield thought the chocolate pieces would melt.

She thought the chocolate pieces would blend into the
cookie dough as baking chocolate does.

But they did not. To her surprise, the chopped pieces
melt, but kept their shape.

And that is how the first chocolate chip cookie was created!

The people at Nestlé liked the chocolate chip cookie made
with their chocolate.

They asked Ms. Wakefield if she would allow them to print
the recipe.

She agreed, and in return received chocolate from Nestlé
for the rest of her life.

KEY WORDS

- piece
- melt
- blend into
- cookie dough
- to one's surprise

- keep (keep-kept-kept)
- shape
- allow
- print
- recipe

- agree
- in return
- receive
- rest

Years later, Nestlé saw that it was a good idea to sell chocolate chips.

Until then, people had to chop up blocks of chocolate, just as Ms. Wakefield had done.

But it was her invention, the chocolate chip cookie, which led to the creation of chocolate chips.

And her cookie recipe? It is still being printed on packages of Nestlé chocolate chips today.

Chocolate chips didn't change the world, but they have provided pleasure for many people.

Another yummy treat that has provided pleasure around the world is the Popsicle. And like the chocolate chip cookie, the Popsicle was invented by accident. The inventor was a boy named Frank Epperson. In 1905, Frank was an 11-year-old who lived in San Francisco, California.

Frank mixed up a syrupy drink of soda water powder and water. For reasons unknown, he left it outside with the stirring stick still in the mixture.

KEY WORDS

- creation
- package
- yummy
- name (+ after)
- mix up (+ with)
- syrupy
- powder

- reason
- unknown
- leave (leave-left-left)
- stir
- stick
- still
- mixture

The weather became very cold. The temperature dropped below freezing that night.

Frank went outside the next morning. He found the drink had frozen with the stick still in it.

Frank tasted it, and enjoyed the world's very first Popsicle!

He didn't call it a Popsicle, though.

He named his frozen treat after himself.

- weather
- temperature
- drop
- below freezing

- freeze (freeze-froze-frozen)
- taste
- very
- though

He took the first part of his last name, Epperson, and a short form of the word icicle.

He put them together and created the word "Epsicle."

Years later, Frank Epperson was grown up with children of his own.

His children called him "Pop." They began asking him for "Pop's 'sicle."

In that manner the "Epsicle" became the "Popsicle."

KEY WORDS

- **last name** (= family name)
- **form**
- **icicle**
- **put together** (put-put-put)
- **grown up**
- **of one's own**
- **in that manner** (= that way)

Did you know that Post-it notes were invented by accident?
Today, Post-its are used in offices and homes around the
world. They sure didn't start out that way.

Post-its came into being when a chemist made a mistake.
In 1968, Spencer Silver was a chemist working for 3M, a
large company. He was asked to invent a strong glue.
By accident, he did just the opposite. He invented a very
weak glue.

The glue was interesting, though.

Even though it could stick and be easily removed, it
continued to stick well after many uses.

The company, 3M, didn't
think much of the weak
glue.
They still needed strong glue.
But Spencer Silver had an idea for
his glue.
He had the idea to cover a bulletin
board with the glue.
People could stick papers to the bulletin
board.
They wouldn't need thumbtacks to attach the papers to the
board.
This wasn't a bad idea, but it didn't catch on.

POP QUIZ

Why was 3M at first unhappy with the Post-it glue?

ⓐ The glue was weak.
ⓑ The glue was too sticky.

KEY WORDS

- office
- start out
- come into being
- chemist
- make a mistake
- work
- glue

- opposite
- even though
- easily
- remove
- use
- think much of
- need

- cover
- bulletin board
- thumbtack
- attach
- catch on

For several years, nothing happened with the glue.

Then one day another 3M chemist, Art Fry, needed a bookmark.

He was frustrated that his paper bookmarks kept sliding out of his book. He kept losing his place.

He remembered the glue and it got him thinking.

What if you put that glue on a paper bookmark? Aha!

Then the bookmark would stick to the pages of the book and not slide out!

Art Fry called Spencer Silver and shared his idea.

Spencer Silver agreed this was a great idea.

They shared the idea with the bosses at 3M.

Can you believe it? They didn't like it!

So again, the glue was set aside.

Which 3M scientist invented the glue on Post-it notes?
ⓐ Spencer Silver
ⓑ Art Fry

KEY WORDS

- several
- bookmark
- frustrated
- keep + *Verb*-ing

- slide
- lose (lose-lost-lost)
- get (get-got-got/gotten)
- share

- boss
- set aside

Several years after they first presented the idea, a different manager at 3M heard the idea. His name was Geoff Nicholson. He believed Post-its were a good idea. Samples were given away.

People tried Post-its for free.

Nicholson wanted to test the market and hopefully build up consumer demand.

And it worked. People wanted more!

So, the company agreed that Post-its were a great idea.

POP QUIZ

What was the position of Geoff Nicholson?
ⓐ manager
ⓑ president

KEY WORDS

- present
- give away (give-gave-given)
- try
- for free
- hopefully
- build up
- consumer demand
- accidental
- store
- throughout
- of course
- result
- such as
- Braille
- circumstance

It took many years after Spencer Silver invented the accidental glue before Post-its were sold in stores throughout the US.

And it took all three men — Spencer Silver, Art Fry, and Geoff Nicholson to make it happen.

Not all inventions are made by accident, of course.

Some inventions are the result of years of hard work, such as Braille.

Braille, like the Popsicle, was invented by a child. But the circumstances were very different.

Comprehension Quiz

A Connect each person to his or her description.

❶ Frank Epperson   •　　• a) innkeeper

❷ Ruth Graves Wakefield • 　　• b) scientist

❸ Alexander Fleming   •　　• c) 11-year-old boy

❹ Silver Spencer   •　　• d) 3M manager

❺ Geoff Nicholson   •　　• e) 3M chemist

B Fill in each blank with the right word below to complete each sentence.

paper	melt	free	frozen

❶ The Popsicle is a tasty ______________ treat.

❷ Ms. Wakefield thought the chocolate pieces would ______________.

❸ Art Fry had the idea to put the glue on a ____________ bookmark.

❹ People tried Post-its for ____________.

Rearrange the following sentences according to the order of events.

❶ a) Frank Epperson's children asked him for "Pop's 'sicle."

b) Frank Epperson named his invention the Epsicle.

c) Frank mixed up a syrupy drink.

d) Frank found the drink frozen with the stick still in it.

_______ → _______ → _______ → _______

❷ a) Art Fry needed a bookmark that didn't fall out of his book.

b) Spencer Silver invented a very weak glue.

c) The company agreed Post-its were a great idea.

d) Spencer Silver was asked to invent a strong glue.

_______ → _______ → _______ → _______

D Choose either "discovered" or "invented" for the underlined part.

❶ Alexander Fleming (discovered / invented) penicillin.

❷ Ms. Wakefield (discovered / invented) chocolate chip cookies.

❸ Post-it notes were (discovered / invented) by accident.

❹ Frank Epperson (discovered / invented) the Popsicle.

Problem Solvers

There is a common phrase, "Necessity is the mother of invention."

This means that if there is something you need or wish to accomplish, you will figure out a way to do it.

In this way you might create a brand-new product or idea.

KEY WORDS

- common phrase
- necessity
- accomplish
- figure out
- brand-new
- product
- work on
- communication
- bear one's name
- blind
- develop
- raised
- dot
- stand for
- letter
- punctuation mark
- touch

▲ Louis Braille's half-length statue (By Arcibel (Own work) [Public domain], via Wikimedia Commons)

That is what Louis Braille did. At the age of only 11 years old, he began working on the communication system that bears his name, Braille.

Louis was blind. He wanted to help himself and other blind people. He developed a system of writing and printing for the blind.

It uses a system of raised dots.

Each dot, or group of dots, stands for a letter, number, or punctuation mark.

A blind person touches the dots to read the writing.

Louis was born in France in 1809.

He was not blind at birth.

He had his vision until the age of three.

One day while playing in his father's workshop, Louis had an accident.

He tried to cut leather with a sharp tool.

His hand slipped. The tool flew up and injured one of his eyes.

After a few days the injury became worse.

He developed an infection in both of his eyes.

This caused the loss of his sight.

Louis became completely blind.

Louis was smart. He was curious and loved to learn.

He didn't let his blindness stop him from doing the things he wanted to do.

He adjusted to his blindness. He still played with his friends. He enjoyed going to school.

He was a creative person. He loved music. He learned to play the cello and the organ. But the thing Louis wanted to do more than anything was to be able to read.

POP QUIZ

What did Louis want to do more than anything?

ⓐ play the cello and the organ
ⓑ be able to read

KEY WORDS

- smart
- curious
- stop + A + *Verb*-ing
- adjust to
- creative
- be able to

Louis learned of a school for the blind. The school was The
Royal Institute for Blind Youth.

Louis moved to Paris and became a student there.

He learned that books for the blind did exist.

The books had large letters

raised off the page.

A blind person could feel

the letters and in that

way read the book.

But the books were

big and bulky.

They were very expensive

to buy. They were so expensive

that the school only had fourteen of them.

KEY WORDS

- learn of
- royal
- institute

- feel
- bulky
- expensive

Louis was excited to read the books.

He understood how to feel each letter. He put the words together to make sentences.

But this way of reading was very slow.

Louis complained that by the time he got to the end of a sentence, he forgot the words at the beginning.

Louis believed he could create a better way for blind people to read.

He thought of devising a "finger alphabet" that would be as easy and fast for blind people to use as the regular alphabet is for sighted people to use.

▲ Charles Barbier

One day a retired French army captain named Charles Barbier visited the school. He told Louis about a coded alphabet he had devised. The coded alphabet was being used by the French army. The code was made up of raised dots and dashes. It was used for sending messages to soldiers at night. The soldiers could feel the dots and dashes with their fingers. By doing this, they did not need light.

KEY WORDS

- retired
- army
- captain
- visit

- coded
- be made up of
- dash (—)
- message

- soldier
- light

This was important, because light was a nighttime danger to the soldiers.

It would give away their position to the enemy.

With the coded alphabet, they could read the message in the dark.

Louis learned to read the code. It was easier than the giant books with the big raised letters.

Even so, it was still slow and hard to use.

The dashes took up a lot of space on the page.

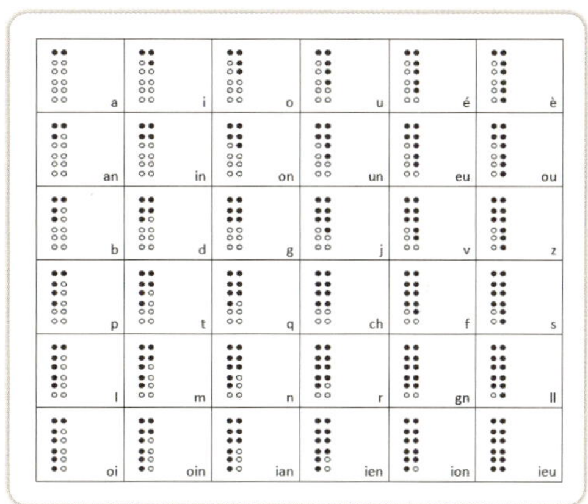

▲ Charles Barbier's Night Code
(By Merayudantia (Own work) [CC BY-SA 3.0
(http://creativecommons.org/licenses/by-sa/3.0)],
via Wikimedia Commons)

One page might have only two sentences on it.

Louis believed he could develop a better way for blind people to read.

- nighttime
- danger
- position
- enemy
- in the dark
- giant
- even so
- take up
- space

Louis wanted his alphabet to include numbers and
punctuation marks.

In his spare time he experimented with a pointed tool called
a stylus.

He used the stylus to punch dots into paper.

He did this to test his alphabet.

The alphabet he created was made of only six dots.

The pattern of the raised dots represented different letters.

Louis used the stylus to punch out a sentence using the
alphabet he created.

He felt the raised dots with his fingertips.

He read from left to right. He read easily and with speed.

He had done it!

He had created a way for the blind to read that was easy
and fast to use.

KEY WORDS

- include
- in one's spare time
- experiment
- pointed
- stylus

- punch
- pattern
- represent
- fingertip
- with speed

Louis spent several years working on his alphabet.

He worked hard to perfect his raised dot system.

He was only 15 years old when he showed his work to the director of his school.

Louis had developed a simple system of reading for the blind. Louis achieved the goal he had set for himself.

KEY WORDS

- **spend** (spend-spent-spent)
- **perfect**
- **director**
- **achieve**

- **goal**
- **set**
- **for oneself**

It would be many years before the system Louis Braille

invented would be accepted throughout the world.

Today, Braille is one of the most widely used methods of

reading and writing for the blind.

Louis Braille wanted to read.

He knew other blind people shared his desire.

He invented a tool to help solve that problem.

Another person who solved problems with his inventions was Benjamin Franklin. 

Benjamin Franklin lived in the 1700s.

He was a printer and an author.

He was an American statesman.

He was a scientist and an inventor, too.

POP QUIZ

What was not one of Benjamin Franklin's jobs?

ⓐ artist

ⓑ writer

KEY WORDS

- accept
- method
- desire
- solve
- problem
- printer
- author
- statesman

Benjamin Franklin invented many things.

He began inventing when he was only 11 years old.

Like many children, he loved to swim. He wanted to swim fast.

He did not think paddling with only his hands and feet made him go fast enough.

He made oval pallets that fit his hands. He made something similar for his feet.

These swim fins helped him swim faster.

KEY WORDS

- paddle
- oval

- pallet
- fit

- similar
- swim fin (*cf.* fin)

Benjamin Franklin
invented the first
bifocal eyeglasses. 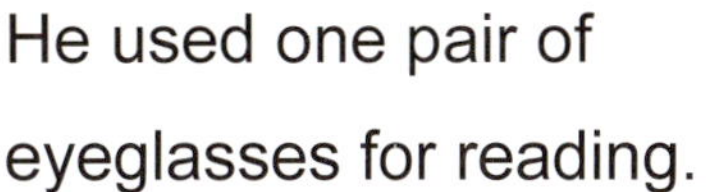
He invented them to
make his life easier.
It frustrated him that
he needed two pairs of
eyeglasses.
He used one pair of
eyeglasses for reading.

He used a second pair for seeing into the distance.
He wished he could see both near and far with only one
pair of glasses.
He thought about his problem and how to fix it.

KEY WORDS

- bifocal
- eyeglasses (= glasses)
- pair
- distance

- near
- far
- fix

Then he had an idea.

He cut the lenses in half.

He took the lens for reading and paired it with the lens for seeing into the distance.

Now when he looked through the lower lens he was able to read.

When he lifted his eyes to the upper lens, he saw in the distance.

His idea of combining differing lenses into a single pair of eyeglasses is still used today.

POP QUIZ

Why did Benjamin Franklin make a new pair of glasses?

ⓐ to read books more closely
ⓑ to read books and see in the distance

KEY WORDS

- in half
- lower
- lift
- upper
- combine
- differing
- lightning

- electricity
- involve
- kite
- Leyden jar
- electric charge
- metal
- string

- fly
- **lightning storm** (= thunderstorm)
- attract
- prove
- **draw** (draw-drew-drawn)

Benjamin Franklin also studied lightning and electricity.

One of his most famous experiments involved a kite, a key, and a Leyden jar.

A Leyden jar is a device for storing an electric charge.

Benjamin Franklin attached a metal key to a kite string.

The kite string was attached to the Leyden jar.

He flew the kite during a lightning storm.

The key attracted the lightning. The electricity went down the string. It was stored in the Leyden jar.

This proved that lightning is a form of electricity.

It also proved that the electricity in lightning could be drawn to metal.

Benjamin Franklin saw this as a way to help keep people safe.

At the time he lived, most buildings were made of wood.

The danger of fire from a lightning strike was high.

It was not uncommon for buildings to catch fire from lightning strikes.

He invented a device to carry the electric current from a lightning strike away from the building.

KEY WORDS

- most
- lightning strike
- uncommon
- catch fire
- carry
- current

This device is called a "lightning rod."

A lightning rod is a pointed rod.

It is attached to the top of a building.

The rod is connected to the ground with the use of a wire.

Lightning strikes the rod. The current is carried through the rod and wire.

The current is delivered into the ground without causing any damage.

Many buildings are still protected in this way.

POP QUIZ

What device helps to protect buildings from lightning strikes?

ⓐ lightning shield
ⓑ lightning rod

KEY WORDS

- lightning rod
- rod
- top
- connect
- ground
- wire
- strike
- deliver
- damage
- protect

Have you ever seen a reaching device called a "long arm?"

As created by Benjamin Franklin, a "long arm" was a long piece of wood with two "fingers" mounted on the end.

All his life, Benjamin Franklin loved to read. He loved books.

But when he became old, reaching books on high shelves became difficult.

KEY WORDS

- reach
- mount
- shelf
- pull
- cable
- grab
- lightweight
- material

He created the "long arm" to reach those books.

He would reach for the book with the "long arm."

Then he would pull a cable to draw the "fingers" together.

The "fingers" would grab the book, and he could bring it down from the shelf.

"Long arms" are still used by people today.

Today, "long arms" are made of plastic or other lightweight materials.

Benjamin Franklin and Louis Braille invented things to solve problems.

Many other inventors have done the same thing.

So do you agree that "necessity is the mother of invention?"

Comprehension Quiz

A Fill in each blank with the right word below to complete each sentence.

dots	invention	easier	blind

❶ Necessity is the mother of ______________.

❷ The Braille system uses a series of raised ______________.

❸ Louis Braille wanted to help himself and other ______________ people.

❹ Benjamin Franklin invented things to make his life ______________.

B Based on the book, mark T for true or F for false.

❶ Louis Braille was born blind. T F

❷ Louis was injured while playing in his father's workshop. T F

❸ Louis was not allowed to go to school. T F

❹ Louis' blindness kept him from doing the things he wanted to do. T F

❺ The Braille system is simple and easy to use. T F

C Choose the best answer to each question.

❶ How did Charles Barbier help Louis invent the Braille system?

a) Charles Barbier helped Louis test his finger alphabet.

b) Charles Barbier taught Louis how to punch dots into paper.

c) Charles Barbier gave Louis a stylus to punch dots into paper.

d) Charles Barbier's code gave Louis the idea for his own finger alphabet.

❷ What do Louis Braille and Benjamin Franklin have in common?

a) They were both child inventors.

b) Both inventors grew up in France.

c) They invented more than one thing.

d) They both lived in the 1800s.

D Write the happenings in Franklin's lab in the right order.

❶ It was proved that electricity is attracted to lightning.

❷ Franklin attached a metal key to a kite string.

❸ The key attracted the lightning.

❹ Franklin flew the kite during a lightning storm.

________ → ________ → ________ → ________

Evolving Inventions

Do you know what it means to take something for granted? It means you are so used to having something that you don't appreciate it.

Some products are so common we take them for granted. One of these is the mobile phone, or the cell phone.

Do you have a cell phone? Even if you don't, your mother and father probably each have one.

Of course you use a cell phone to call and talk to people. But it has other uses, too.

Maybe you play games on your cell phone. Perhaps you listen to music. Or you might access the Internet with it.

All these uses didn't come with the very first cell phone. That first cell phone could only be used for calls. Boring, right? 

KEY WORDS

- evolve
- take A for granted
- be used to
- appreciate

- mobile phone (= cell phone)
- probably
- listen to
- access

The cell phone is an example of an invention that evolved.
That means that it began as one thing, and changed into
something more complex.

So how did it begin? Let's go back to the 1800s and see
how it started.

Sometimes inventors have similar ideas.
That makes it tough to know who had the idea first. The

telephone is one of these
inventions.

In 1871, Antonio Meucci
designed a talking telegraph.
But he had some bad luck and
his invention was not patented.

▲ Antonio Meucci
(By Unknown, 1878.
See page for author [Public domain or Public
domain], via Wikimedia Commons)

- change into
- complex
- go back to
- tough

- design
- telegraph
- patent

A patent is a legal document.
It gives the inventor the right to
claim ownership of the invention.
Then on February 14, 1876,
Elisha Gray and Alexander
Graham Bell both filed for
patents.
Both men had invented a similar
device.
But Bell was faster. He was the
5th person to file for a patent
that day. Gray was the 39th.

▲ Elisha Gray
(By Unknown, 1878-1879.
See page for author [Public domain], via
Wikimedia Commons)

POP QUIZ

Who came earlier to file for a patent?
ⓐ Elisha Gray
ⓑ Alexander Graham Bell

KEY WORDS

- legal
- document
- right
- claim
- ownership
- file for

For this reason, Bell's request received the patent.

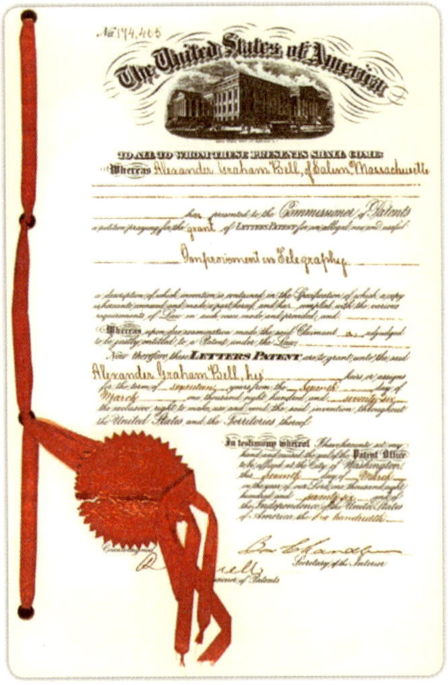

▲ a charter given to Alexander Graham Bell
for the invention of the telephone
(By U.S.P.T.O., March 1876
[Public domain or Public domain],
via Wikimedia Commons)

This raised the question of who really invented the telephone. There were many legal questions and arguments. In the end, Alexander Graham Bell got the credit for inventing the telephone.

POP QUIZ

Which statement below is correct?

ⓐ Elisha Gray won the patent for inventing the telephone.
ⓑ Alexander Graham Bell won the patent for inventing the telephone.

KEY WORDS

- request
- raise
- argument

- in the end
- get (the) credit for

Alexander Graham Bell was a scientist and an inventor. He studied the human voice. He also worked in schools for the deaf as a teacher. He studied ways of communication for the deaf so he could further develop his own system. Bell experimented with sound. He believed there was a way to transmit the human voice over wires. He studied physics and other sciences.

▲ Alexander Graham Bell
(See page for author [Public domain], via Wikimedia Commons)

KEY WORDS

- voice
- deaf
- further
- sound
- transmit
- physics

In 1875 he hired an assistant, Thomas Watson, to help him.

The men worked for a year testing Bell's ideas.

Then, on March 10, 1876, they had success.

While testing their invention, Bell heard sounds through the wire.

This encouraged him and he spoke these words: "Watson, come here, I want you."

Watson did hear Bell's voice.

This was the first time voice was transmitted over wire.

Bell's invention worked!

- hire
- assistant
- have success
- encourage

Bell introduced the world to his telephone soon after.

He demonstrated it at the Centennial Exhibition in

Philadelphia in 1876. 

This was the largest world's fair at the time.

The President of the United States, Ulysses S. Grant,

invited the Emperor of Brazil, Dom Pedro II, to attend.

Dom Pedro had an interest in science and technology.

He met Alexander Graham Bell.

They talked about Bell's telephone.

POP QUIZ

Where did Bell introduce his new invention to the world?

ⓐ at a world fair
ⓑ at his lab

KEY WORDS

- introduce
- demonstrate
- centennial
- fair
- president

- emperor
- attend
- have an interest in
- technology

When Bell demonstrated

his invention, Dom Pedro was the first to hear it.

Bell stood 91.4 meters away in the main building and

spoke into his device.

He recited the words from Shakespeare's *Hamlet*.

His voice carried over the wire.

When Dom Pedro heard it, he was surprised.

He exclaimed, "My God, it talks!"

KEY WORDS

- recite
- exclaim
- my God
- possible

- popularity
- the turn of the century
- million
- in use (↔ not in use, out of use)

People had never heard such a thing before.

It was now possible to speak over a wire.

It was possible to talk to people who were very far away.

You can imagine how excited people became.

This was a big invention!

Over the next 25 years the popularity of the telephone grew.

By the turn of the century there were more than one million telephones in use.

By 1938, there were 30 million phones in use.

▲ a telephone in the 1930s

POP QUIZ

How many telephones were in use by 1938?

ⓐ one million
ⓑ 30 million

Next came mobile phones. Mobile phones use radio frequencies to transmit sound.

This transmitting sound over radio frequencies was a new innovation in the mid 1940s.

Groups of scientists working together developed the idea.

On June 17, 1946 the mobile phone was tested for the first time.

A truck driver made a call from his vehicle. The phone device was attached to the dashboard with a cord. The first mobile call was made.

Early mobile phones were more like two-way radios. They allowed people like truck drivers and emergency service workers to make important phone calls.

KEY WORDS

- frequency
- innovation
- mid
- for the first time

- vehicle
- dashboard
- cord
- two-way radio

- emergency service
- make a phone call

The idea of mobile phones operating in a different way came in 1947.

D. H. Ring and W. Rae Young worked for Bell Labs. They developed the idea of using a network of wireless towers. Their diagram of towers resembled a biological cell.

The term "cellular" network came from this.

Their idea was good, but the system didn't work well.

It wasn't until the 1960s that others perfected this idea. They made it work using electronics and computers.

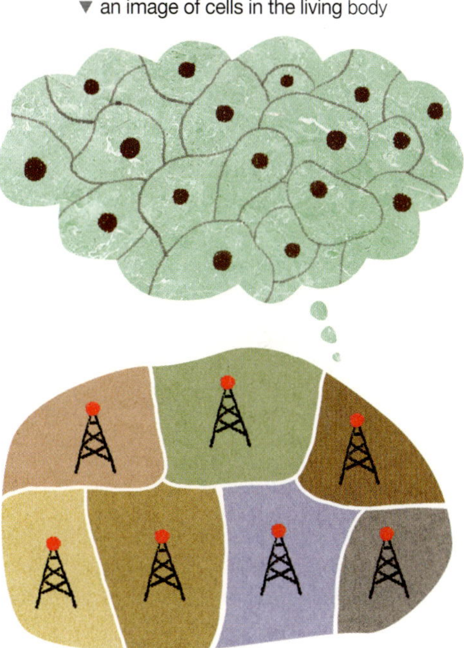

▲ an image of a wireless tower network

As a result, in 1973 the first cellular phone call was made.
Because mobile phones use the cellular system, they are
sometimes called "cell phones."
A man named Martin Cooper devised the first handheld
mobile phone.
Compared to the mobile phones of today, it looked very
different.
For one thing, it was big. It was so big, it was nicknamed
"The Brick."

Compare it to today's iPhone 6 Plus:

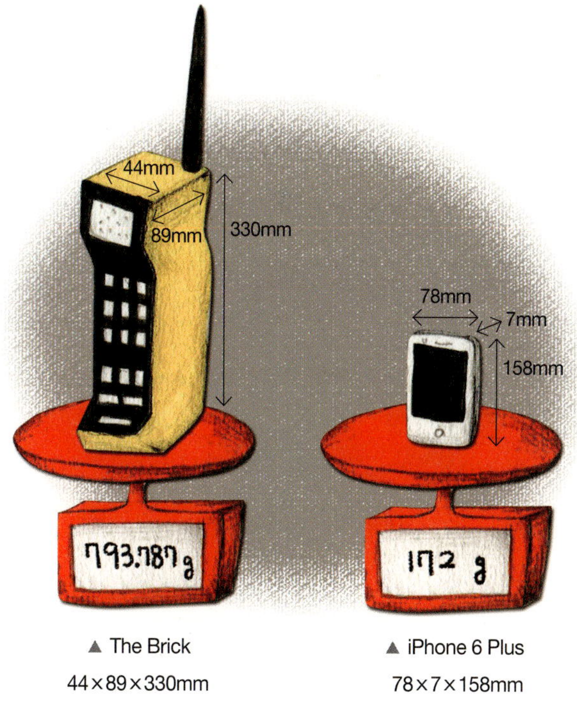

▲ The Brick
44×89×330mm

▲ iPhone 6 Plus
78×7×158mm

Can you imagine carrying "The Brick" in your pocket?

There was no display screen like we have today.

It had only a punch keypad.

- as a result
- handheld
- compared to
- for one thing
- nickname
- brick
- display
- punch
- keypad

Technology has advanced since the first mobile phones.
Digital technology has allowed for the development of today's smart phones.
People now do much more than talk on their cell phones.
They take photos, listen to music, watch movies, and access the Internet.

Can you think of other uses for mobile phones?
What do you think Alexander Graham Bell would say if he were alive to see today's phones?
Would he be surprised at the way his invention evolved?

Another invention that evolved over time is the television.

Unlike the telephone, the television was not invented by one person.

It took many different people to develop the television.

Some worked together. Others worked alone.

It was the combination of these efforts that led to the development of the television.

The basis for all modern televisions came from the mind of 21-year-old Philo Farnsworth.

In 1927 he was the first to demonstrate an electronic television.

KEY WORDS

- unlike
- alone
- combination
- effort
- basis
- mind

He used a cathode ray tube
(CRT) for transmission.
A CRT is a tube that produces
the image people watch.
You may have heard of the
CRT.

▲ CRT monitor

▲ LCD monitor

The CRT used to be widely
used in computer monitors as
well. Aha!
Some CRTs are still in use, but
new computers most often use
a liquid crystal display (LCD).

POP QUIZ

What year were programs first broadcast in color?
ⓐ 1953
ⓑ 1966

KEY WORDS

- cathode ray tube (CRT)
- transmission
- tube
- produce
- most often

- liquid crystal display
- reality
- at first
- available

In the 1920's Philo used a CRT for his television.

It is Philo's system that is the basis for all modern televisions.

Philo got the idea for his television when he was only 14 years old.

It took him seven years to make his invention a reality.

At first, television only displayed black and white images.

Color television became available in 1953. Most programs were still transmitted in black and white, though.

It wasn't until 1966 that television programs changed to color.

▲ a receiver for a satellite TV

Since TV began being broadcast in color, there have been many other improvements.
In the 1970s, cable television and satellite television allowed for more channels.

Today, microprocessors and microelectronic devices allow graphic displays and videos to be easily watched.
Television screens have also improved.
Old TVs used the CRT which was very bulky. This meant TVs were quite big.

- broadcast
- improvement
- satellite
- channel
- microprocessor
- microelectronic device
- graphic display
- quite

- light-emitting diode
- benefit
- thin
- weigh
- furthermore
- clear
- energy efficient

These days TV screens use different technologies like plasma, LCD, and light-emitting diode (LED) technology. LCD TVs offer many

benefits over the old CRT. For one thing, LCD screens are much thinner.

LCD technology also allows for a wider screen.

A CRT for a large screen TV would simply be too big.

It would take up too much space and also would be too heavy.

LCD and LED screens take up much less space and weigh less, too.

Furthermore, LCD and LED screens create a clearer image.

They are also more energy efficient than CRTs.

POP QUIZ

Which of the following statements is true?

ⓐ LCD TVs are bulkier than CRT TVs.

ⓑ CRT TVs are bulkier than LCD TVs.

Some TVs today even display 3D (three-dimensional) images.

This requires the use of special glasses. The glasses adjust the image. They create the illusion of 3D.

What do you think the early inventors of the television would think about today's TVs?

Would Philo Farnsworth be surprised to see how the invention he dreamed up as a boy has evolved?

KEY WORDS

- three dimensional
- require
- adjust
- illusion
- dream up

The first remote control device for changing channels was developed in 1950.

It was not wireless. It was attached to the television with a cable. It was called "Lazy Bones."

The name meant that the user could be lazy and not get up to change the channel.

The company that invented the Lazy Bones remote thought it would be popular.

They expected many people to buy it.

But the Lazy Bones was not as widely used as they had hoped. People complained of tripping over the cord.

KEY WORDS

- remote control device
  (= remote control)
- lazy bones
- lazy
- get up
- remote
- expect
- trip over

Today's
remote controls
use infrared
technology. _Aha!_
They do not require a
cord.
The infrared remotes work by
using a low-frequency light beam.
Human eyes cannot see it.
But the receiver inside the television can see it.
This type of wireless remote control is now a standard
feature on most electronics.
Like the telephone, the television has evolved over the
years.
What new improvements do you imagine in the future?
What type of telephone and television do you see in the
future?

While you were reading, did you notice that the words television and telephone are similar?

They share the same prefix.

A prefix is a word placed before another.

Both television and telephone begin with "tele."

"Tele" means "from a long distance."

This prefix is used in many words.

In addition to television and telephone, the words telegraph, telecast, and telescope also employ this prefix.

Perhaps you can think of others.

The common meaning for all these words is "from a long distance."

POP QUIZ

What does the prefix "tele" mean?

ⓐ from a long distance
ⓑ with the use of a wire

KEY WORDS

- prefix
- place
- in addition to
- telecast
- telescope
- employ

Chapter Three

Comprehension Quiz

A Fill in each blank with the right word below to complete each sentence.

culture evolved distance technology

❶ The prefix "tele" means "from a long ______________."

❷ The telephone and television are both inventions that ______________ over time.

❸ The telephone and television changed human ______________.

❹ ______________ has improved the telephone and television.

B Choose the best answer to each question.

❶ Which of the following men assisted Alexander Graham Bell in his research?

a) Elisha Gray   b) Geoff Nicholson

c) Antonio Meucci   d) Thomas Watson

❷ Which word does NOT describe Alexander Graham Bell?

a) inventor   b) teacher

c) scientist   d) chemist

 Choose the best two answers to each question.

❶ How are telephones and televisions similar?

a) They transmit over long distances.

b) They were both invented in the 1800s.

c) They evolved over time.

d) They both use LCD technology.

❷ Why did LCD TVs replace CRT TVs?

a) LCD screens can be much wider than CRT screens.

b) LCD screens are thinner than CRT screens.

c) LCD TVs are more bulky than CRT TVs.

d) LCD technology creates a darker image.

D Choose the inventor related to the given words and phrases.

❶ voice over wire   **Bell / Farnsworth**

❷ CRT   **Bell / Farnsworth**

❸ Centennial Exhibition   **Bell / Farnsworth**

❹ TV   **Bell / Farnsworth**

Kids' Inventions

In chapter one, we saw how the Popsicle was invented.

Frank Epperson invented the Popsicle by accident.

But other kids have invented things on purpose.

Like Louis Braille, these kids saw a need for something.

They thought of an invention to satisfy the need.

In 1858, 15-year-old Chester Greenwood invented earmuffs.

He was ice skating one day.

It was very cold outside.

He wrapped his wool scarf around his ears to warm them.

The wool itched.

The scarf was heavy and wouldn't stay put.

Then Chester had a great idea.

He used wire to make two connected loops.

He asked his grandmother to sew fur on them.

Chester had solved his problem of cold ears.

- on purpose
- satisfy
- earmuffs
- wrap
- wool
- scarf

- warm
- itch
- stay put
- loop
- **sew** (sew-sewed-sewed/sewn)
- fur

He named his invention Greenwood's Champion Ear Protectors. His invention became popular.

During World War I, soldiers used Chester's invention to keep warm.

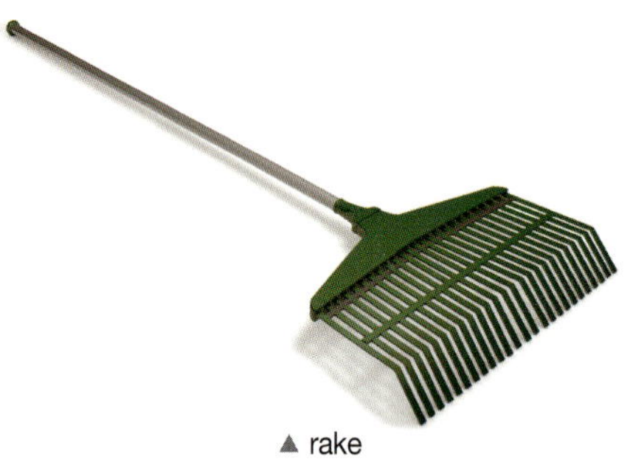
▲ rake

Earmuffs are still popular today.

Chester didn't stop with earmuffs.

He invented more than 100 things in his lifetime.

These included a steel-toothed rake, a wide-bottomed kettle, and a folding bed.

Have you ever
jumped on a
trampoline? If so,
you owe your fun to
George Nissen.
In 1930, George
Nissen was just 16

years old when he thought up the idea for the trampoline.
George had been to the circus.
He saw the trapeze artists
perform.
George wanted to bounce
the way the trapeze artists
did when they fell into their nets.

trapeze artist ▶

He went home and began working on his new idea.

In his parents' garage he built the first trampoline.

He strapped a canvas sheet to a rectangular steel frame.

He called it a "bouncing rig."

It worked. He was able to bounce on it, but it was not as springy as he wanted it to be.

George decided to keep working on his invention.

While in college George teamed up with his gymnastics coach, Larry Griswold.

Together, they improved on George's bouncing rig.

George named his invention after a Spanish word.

The Spanish word "trampolin" means "springboard."

George took his invention all over the world.

The trampoline has been used for more than just fun.

Trampolines were used to train American and Soviet astronauts.

Trampoline training gave the astronauts experience in body positioning and flight.

Gymnasts use the trampoline for training.

And at the 2000 Olympic Games in Sydney, Australia, trampoline became an Olympic sport.

KEY WORDS

- garage
- strap
- canvas
- sheet
- rectangular
- steel frame
- rig
- springy
- college
- team up with
- gymnastics
- springboard
- train
- Soviet
- astronaut
- experience
- flight
- gymnast

Another great kid inventor is Becky Schroeder.

In 1972, Becky was 10 years old. Becky's mother was shopping inside a store.

Becky waited in the car so she could do her math schoolwork. It began to get dark outside.

Becky didn't have a flashlight.

She wished there was some way to light up the paper so she could see to do her schoolwork.

It was then that the idea for a Glo-sheet came to her.

She knew she wanted to light up paper in the dark.

She just had to figure out how to do it.

That night Becky couldn't stop thinking of her idea.

She thought of all the things that glow in the dark.

She thought of fireflies (lightning bugs).

She thought of some of her glow-in-the-dark toys.

The next day she went to the store and bought phosphorescent paint.

If something is phosphorescent, that means it stores energy from the light.

When it is dark, the energy radiates as a glow.

Becky brought the paint home and began experimenting.

POP QUIZ

What do fireflies and phosphorescent paint have in common?

ⓐ They glow in the light.
ⓑ They glow in the dark.

KEY WORDS

- **math** (= mathematics)
- **schoolwork**
- **get dark**
- **flashlight**
- **light up**
- **then**
- **Glo-sheet**
- **firefly** (= lightning bug)
- **phosphorescent**
- **radiate**

Becky took the paint and paper into a darkened room.

She put the paper on an acrylic clipboard.

She experimented with the paint.

She learned that the paper didn't need to glow.

The clipboard could glow, and it would light up the paper.

Over the next two years, Becky continued to experiment.

She found her invention worked better with batteries to

generate the glow.

Becky Schroeder's invention, made public when she was

12 years old, has many helpful uses. (Aha!)

Photographers use it while in the darkroom developing

photographs.

Doctors and nurses use it in patients' rooms at night.

Movie reviewers use it in darkened theaters.

POP QUIZ

How old was Becky when her Glo-sheet made public?

ⓐ 12 years old
ⓑ 10 years old

KEY WORDS

- darken
- acrylic
- clipboard
- generate
- make public

- photographer
- darkroom
- patient's room (*cf*. patient)
- reviewer
- theater

Since young
Becky developed
the Glo-sheet,
other inventors
have applied
the idea to other
things.
There are golf
balls that glow in
the dark.
A man made a

whole bicycle that glows in the dark.
Someone else invented toilet paper that glows in the dark!
The glow-in-the-dark toilet paper was discontinued.
Can you guess why? Because if you used it, your bottom
would glow!

- apply
- toilet paper
- discontinue
- guess
- bottom

Krysta Morlan invented the Cast Cooler.

Krysta suffers from an illness called cerebral palsy.

This illness has forced her to have many surgeries.

In 1998 the 14-year-old was unhappy because of the casts she was wearing on her arms and legs.

The casts irritated her skin. 

They were very uncomfortable.

Krysta got the idea for a device to blow air under the cast.

The air would cool her skin. She invented the Cast Cooler.

It is a device with a modified aquarium pump that uses a nine-volt battery to operate.

She won awards with her invention.

POP QUIZ

What illness does Krysta Morlan suffer from?

ⓐ cerebral palsy
ⓑ bell's palsy

KEY WORDS

- cast
- cooler
- suffer from
- illness
- cerebral palsy
- force
- surgery
- irritate

- blow
- cool
- skin
- modified
- aquarium
- win (win-won-won)
- award

After inventing the Cast Cooler, Krysta invented a water
bike.

Due to her illness, she must do hours of physical therapy in
a pool.

She likes the water, but finds the therapy to be boring.

The bike she invented makes her therapy fun.

It is made of floating materials. It is semi-submerged.

This means it is only under the water part of the way.

It has foot pedals and fins. It doesn't look like a road bike.

It looks a little like a drag car.

Krysta pedals the water bike in the water and steers it with
a rudder.

Krysta hopes her invention will help other people the way it
helps her.

KEY WORDS

- due to
- physical therapy
- pool
- float
- semi-submerged
- part of the way
- pedal
- drag car
- steer
- rudder

In 2005, at the age of
10, Taylor Hernandez
invented Magic
Sponge Blocks.
The blocks are a
special toy for small
children.

They are big blocks made of sponge.

There are magnets inside of them to hold them together.

A child can build with them.

If the blocks fall over, no one gets hurt!

And they can be pressed together like pancakes for easy

storage.

KEY WORDS

- magnet
- hold

- fall over
- get hurt

- press
- storage

In 2010, 13-year-old Hart Main's sister was selling scented candles for her school.

Hart teased her about the "girly" candles because they smelled sweet and flowery.

He said there should be scented candles with "manly" odors.

Hart was joking, but decided it was a good idea.

Using money he had earned as a newspaper delivery boy, he bought wax and many different scents online.

He experimented with the scents until he was happy with the "manly" smells.

POP QUIZ

How did Hart Main earn money to develop his scented candles?

ⓐ as a busboy in a restaurant
ⓑ as a newspaper delivery boy

KEY WORDS

- scented
- candle
- tease
- girly

- smell
- flowery
- manly
- odor

- joke
- delivery
- wax
- scent

He made candles that smell like coffee. He made candles that smell like fresh cut grass. He made candles that smell like a new baseball mitt.

He calls his candles ManCans.

Hart decided to use empty soup cans to make his candles. This led to another idea. It was an idea that would help other people.

To empty the soup cans, Hart Main donates all the soup to soup kitchens (places that feed the poor).

The soup kitchens use the soup. They wash and return the empty cans to Hart.

Hart reuses the cans for his ManCans.

In that way, with the purchase of a ManCan, the buyer not only receives a scented candle, but helps to feed those less fortunate.

KEY WORDS

- fresh
- grass
- baseball mitt
- empty
- donate
- feed
- the poor (*cf.* poor)
- wash
- return
- reuse
- purchase
- buyer
- fortunate (↔ unfortunate)

SOUP
SOUP
SOUP
SOUP
MAN
CAN
MAN
CAN
MAN
MAN
CAN
MAN

So what do you think about all of these inventions?

Some came about through years of hard work.

Some required lots of experimentation, time, and more than one person to develop.

Still others resulted from surprising accidents.

As different as all of these inventions are, they all have something in common.

Every invention, no matter what it is, needs this one thing.

It is something very important.

Can you guess what that is?

KEY WORDS

- come about
- experimentation
- result from

- have ~ in common
- disability
- physical

Every invention ever made required an inventor.

An inventor can be anyone.

An inventor can be someone with a disability, like Louis Braille, or an illness, like Krysta Morlan.

An inventor can be someone who is not suffering from any physical problems, like Frank Epperson or Hart Main.

An inventor can be a man or a woman, a boy or a girl.

An inventor can be YOU!

POP QUIZ

What do all inventions have in common?

ⓐ an inventor

ⓑ a patent

Chapter Four

Comprehension Quiz

A Connect each invention and a related word correctly.

❶ trampoline ·   · a) bouncing rig

❷ Glo-sheet ·   · b) candles

❸ Cast Cooler ·   · c) phosphorescent

❹ ManCan ·   · d) cool air

B Mark T for true or F for false.

❶ Chester Greenwood invented a wooden-toothed rake. T F

❷ Earmuffs are still popular today. T F

❸ George Nissen thought up the idea for the trampoline after a trip to the circus. T F

❹ Hart decided to use empty soup cans to make his candles. T F

❺ Not all inventions need an inventor. T F

C Rearrange the following sentences according to the order of events.

❶ a) Becky brought phosphorescent paint home and began experimenting.

b) Becky wanted to light up paper so she could see to do her schoolwork.

c) Becky thought of all the things that glow in the dark.

d) She found her invention worked better with batteries to generate the glow.

_______ → _______ → _______ → _______

❷ a) Hart said there should be scented candles with "manly" odors.

b) Hart donated all the soup to soup kitchens.

c) Hart teased his sister about selling "girly" candles.

d) Hart bought wax and many different scents online.

_______ → _______ → _______ → _______

D Which one do the Glo–sheet and Cast Cooler NOT have in common?

a) Both were discovered by a child.

b) Both use batteries to operate.

c) Both inventors were girls.

d) Both have helpful uses.

Fill in the blanks to review the story.

Title: ___________________

Chapter 1:
- Main Idea: Some discoveries and inventions were made by accident.
- Alexander Fleming – p___________
  Ruth Graves Wakefield – c___________ c___________ cookie
  Frank Epperson – P___________
  Spencer Silver, Art Fry, and Geoff Nicholson – ___________-it

Chapter 2 :
- Main Idea: Some useful inventions were created to make l___________ easier.
- Louis Braille – B___________
  Benjamin Franklin – b___________ eyeglasses, l___________ r___________, and long arm

Chapter 3 :
- Main Idea: Some inventions began as one thing and c___________ into something more complex.
- Alexander Graham Bell – ___________
  D. H. Ring and W. Rae Young – n___________ of wireless towers
  Philo Farnsworth – t___________

Chapter 4 :
- Main Idea: Some useful things were invented by ___________.
- Chester Greenwood – e___________, steel-toothed rake, and f___________ bed
  George Nissen – t___________
  Becky Schroeder – G___________-s___________
  Krysta Morlan – C___________ Cooler and w___________ b___________
  Taylor Hernandez – Magic S___________ B___________
  Hart Main – M___________

Let's Think & Talk

Think about the following questions and answer them freely.

❶ Among the various discoveries and inventions in the book, which one do you think is the most important in human history and why?

❷ Among the inventions in the book, which one do you use the most in your daily life and think is the most important?

❸ If you had the technology and money to be able to invent anything that you wanted, what would you invent? Tell us how the invention would help us in our daily lives.

❹ What is most important to be a good inventor? Tell us what personality or ability an inventor has to have.

Let's Review the Story

Title: **Great Inventions around Us**

Chapter 1:
- Main Idea: Some discoveries and inventions were made by accident.
- Alexander Fleming – **penicillin**
  Ruth Graves Wakefield – **chocolate chip** cookie
  Frank Epperson – **Popsicle**
  Spencer Silver, Art Fry, and Geoff Nicholson – **Post**-it

Chapter 2:
- Main Idea: Some useful inventions were created to make **life** easier.
- Louis Braille – **Braille**
  Benjamin Franklin – **bifocal** eyeglasses, **lightning rod**, and long arm

Chapter 3:
- Main Idea: Some inventions began as one thing and **changed** into something more complex.
- Alexander Graham Bell – **telephone**
  D. H. Ring and W. Rae Young – **network** of wireless towers
  Philo Farnsworth – **television**

Chapter 4:
- Main Idea: Some useful things were invented by **kids**.
- Chester Greenwood – **earmuffs**, steel-toothed rake, and **folding** bed
  George Nissen – **trampoline**
  Becky Schroeder – **Glo**-**sheet**
  Krysta Morlan – **Cast** Cooler and **water bike**
  Taylor Hernandez – Magic **Sponge Blocks**
  Hart Main – **ManCan**

After-reading Test

- **Great Inventions around Us**

- **Level 4**

- **29 Questions**

  (Vocabulary 7 / Reading Comprehension 16 /

  Sentence Structure & Grammar 6)

※ Choose the word which has the similar meaning. (1~2)

1. therapy
   ① penicillin   ② cure
   ③ mold   ④ infection

2. semi-submerged
   ① removable   ② lightweight
   ③ partly underwater ④ perfectly fit

3. Which has an opposite meaning of "accidental"?
   ① planned   ② early
   ③ strong   ④ enjoyable

4. Choose one of the following to complete the sentence.

   > To take something for granted means _____________________.

   ① you don't like it very much
   ② you don't have to share it
   ③ you don't appreciate it
   ④ you may use it for free

※ Choose the right word for each blank. (5~6)

5.
   > He was frustrated that his paper bookmarks ___________ sliding out of
   > his book.

   ① went   ② got
   ③ kept   ④ took

6.

> Have you ever seen a reaching ____________ called a "long arm?"

① strike   ② patent
③ innovation   ④ device

7. What is the common word for the two blanks?

> • But other kids have invented things ____________ purpose.
> • He went home and began working ____________ his new idea.

① on   ② by
③ for   ④ with

8. Which is correct?

① An invention is something a person builds by himself.
② An invention never existed until someone imagined and created it.
③ An invention is discovered in nature.
④ An invention already existed and was recently found.

9. What mistake led to the invention of Post-its?

① The glue was stronger than 3M wanted.
② The glue was weaker than 3M wanted.
③ The glue would not stick to anything.
④ The glue glowed in the dark.

10. Which word does NOT describe Louis Braille?

① smart   ② blind
③ French   ④ statesman

11. Which word best fits in the blank?

> Each letter of the alphabet Louis Braille invented was made of only
> _____________ dots.

① eight   ② seven

③ nine   ④ six

12. Why did the French army use a coded alphabet? Choose two answers.

① It was easier to read and write than the regular alphabet.

② The soldiers could read messages in the dark.

③ It helped the soldiers keep their position hidden from the enemy.

④ Charles Barbier invented it and wanted to test it.

13. Which of the following was NOT part of Benjamin Franklin's lightning experiment?

① Leyden jar   ② lightning rod

③ lightning storm   ④ kite string

14. Why did Benjamin Franklin invent bifocal eyeglasses?

① He wanted to protect his eyes in the sun.

② He wanted to see both near and far with only one pair of glasses.

③ He hoped to win the patent for eyeglasses.

④ He lost his eyeglasses and needed another pair.

15. Which word describes Alexander Graham Bell?

① assistant   ② chemist

③ teacher   ④ emperor

16. What were the first words Bell transmitted over wire?
① "Watson, can you hear me?"
② "Watson, are you there?"
③ "Watson, come here, I want you."
④ "Watson, hello, I am here."

17. Which of the following phrases does NOT describe today's remote control devices?
① uses infrared technology
② attaches to the TV with a cord
③ wireless
④ standard on most electronic devices

18. Why was the "Lazy Bones" NOT as popular as expected?
① It was easy to use.
② People complained it was too bulky.
③ People complained of tripping over the cord.
④ It broke too easily.

19. Which two sentences are correct about George Nissen?
① George Nissen was just 16 years old when he thought up the idea for the trampoline.
② George Nissen was just 18 years old when he invented the trampoline.
③ George Nissen thought up the idea for the trampoline after a trip to the circus.
④ George Nissen invented the trampoline after a trip to watch Olympic gymnasts.

20. How did the trampoline help train astronauts?
① Trampoline training gave the astronauts experience in bouncing up and down.
② Trampoline training gave the astronauts experience in body positioning and flight.
③ Trampoline training gave the astronauts a way to have fun.
④ Trampoline training taught the astronauts how to be gymnasts.

21. Why are Magic Sponge Blocks very safe toy for children?
    ① If the blocks fall on children, they don't get hurt.
    ② Children never trip and fall over them.
    ③ There are magnets inside of them to hold them together.
    ④ Children never throw them at each other.

22. Why did Krysta Morlan invent the water bike?
    ① to keep her skin cool
    ② to make her pool physical therapy fun
    ③ to keep the cast hard
    ④ to make it easier to float

23. Which of the following is NOT a ManCan scent?
    ① fresh cut grass   ② flowers
    ③ baseball mitt   ④ coffee

※ Choose the wrong part of each sentence. (24~25)

24. The wheel has make life easier for humans.
               ①   ②   ③   ④

25. Another person who solved problems with his inventions were
                   ①   ②   ③   ④
Benjamin Franklin.

※ Choose the correct sentence. (26~27)

26. ① He used one pairs of eyeglass for reading.
　　② He used one pairs of eyeglasses for reading.
　　③ He used one pair of eyeglass for reading.
　　④ He used one pair of eyeglasses for reading.

27. ① They were too expensive to the school only had fourteen of them.
　　② They were so expensive that the school only had fourteen of them.
　　③ They were so expensive if the school only had fourteen of them.
　　④ They were too expensive if the school only had fourteen of them.

※ Choose the correct word or phrase for each blank. (28~29)

28. The CRT ____________ widely used in computer monitors as well.

① used　　　　　　　　　　② used be
③ used to　　　　　　　　　④ used to be

29. Every invention, ____________ what it is, needs this one thing.

① no matter　　　　　　　② whether
③ if　　　　　　　　　　　④ not only

Lisa Ricard Claro

Lisa Ricard Claro is an award-winning short story author with published articles and stories spanning multiple media, including two adult fiction novels and a third scheduled for publication. She resides in Atlanta, Georgia with her husband, two dogs and two cats, and dreams of one day living at the beach. Writing is Lisa's passion, and she loves creating fiction and nonfiction stories for both adults and children.

Great Inventions around Us

Written by Lisa Ricard Claro
Illustrated by Miseon Hwang

First Published in March 2016

Editorial Manager: Juyon Choi
Editors: Juyon Choi, Myungjin Kim, Kyunghee Jang, Jiyeong Park
Designers: Eunhee Lee, Elim
Cover Designer: Eunhee Lee

Published and distributed by

Darakwon Bldg., 64-1 Jandari-ro, Mapo-gu, Seoul, Korea 04031
Tel: 82-2-736-2031(ext. 250)   Fax: 82-2-732-2037
Homepage: www.ihappyhouse.co.kr
Publisher: Kyudo Chung

ISBN: 978-89-6653-293-3 18740 / 978-89-6653-156-1 18740(set)

[Components]
• 1 Audio CD (Recording Studio: Aram)
• Answer Keys & Korean Translation: Free download at www.ihappyhouse.co.kr